D0796201

The Guessing Machine

Predicting Sequences

by Lynn Maslen Kertell
pictures by Sue Hendra and John R. Maslen

Scholastic Inc.

New York • Toronto • London • Auckland • Sydney • Mexico City • New Delhi • Hong Kong • Buenos Aires

A Guessing Machine came to town.
What does a Guessing Machine do?

It guesses what comes
next. You can guess, too.

Seth started to stack the blocks.

You can guess with the Guessing
Machine. What happened next?

Did you guess that Seth
built a block tower? He did!

Here's a surprise! Then
Tanner knocked it down!

It was raining. Sally put on
her rain boots, coat, and hat.

Can you and the Guessing Machine
guess what happened next?

Did you guess that Sally went
out to play in the rain? She did!

Surprise! Then the rain stopped. Seth and Tanner came out to play, too.

What did Sally, Seth, and
Tanner do next? Guess!